Harvest Time

by Kelly Gaffney

We eat lots of foods
that come from plants.

The plants often grow on big farms.
They are called crops.
When the crops are ready to eat,
they have to be picked.
Picking a crop is called harvesting.

3

There are lots of ways
to harvest a crop.
Some crops are picked by hand.
And other crops are harvested
with a *machine*.
Machines can help the farmer to harvest
the crops quickly.
Some crops can go bad
if they are not picked quickly.

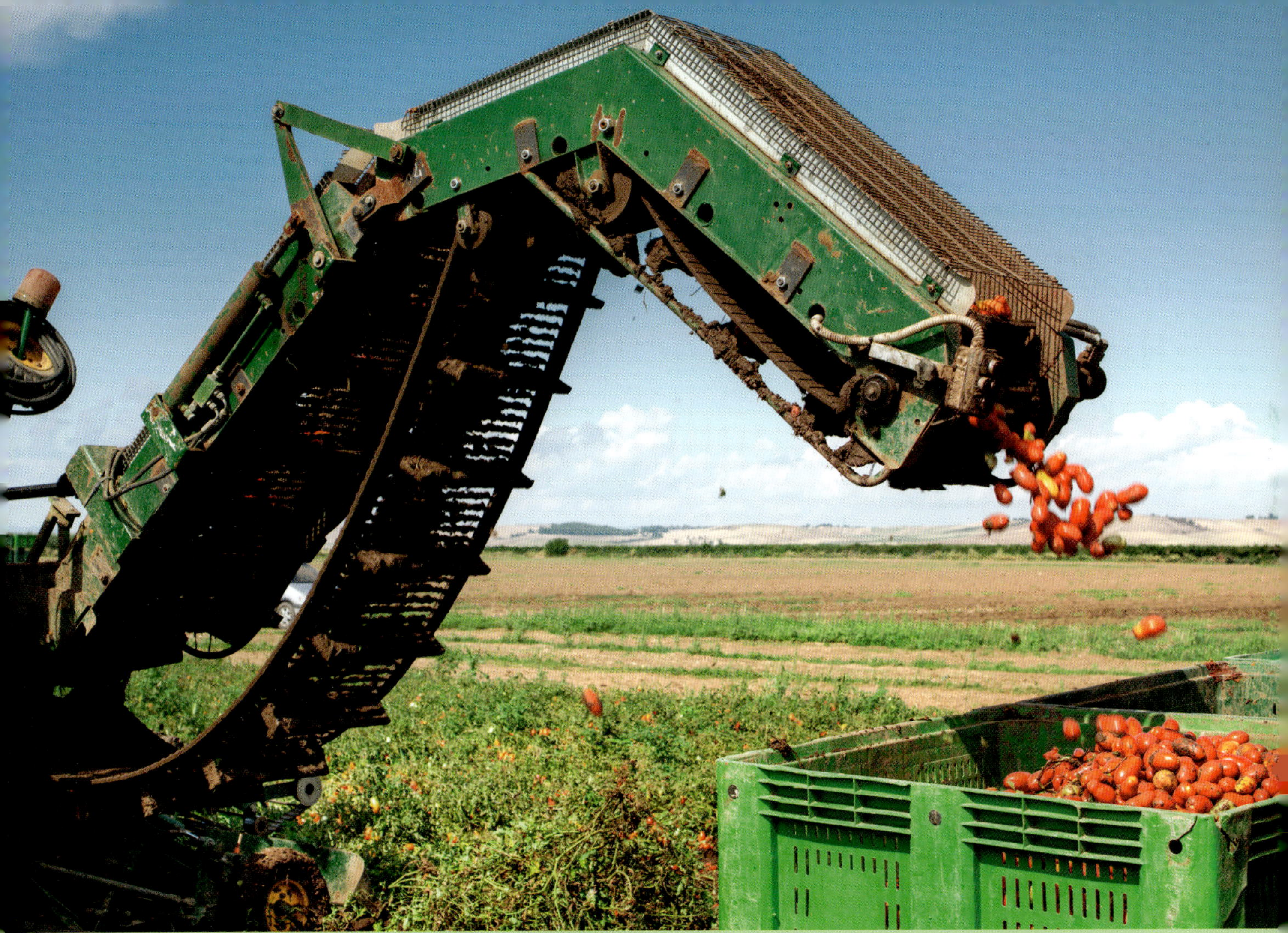

There are lots of apples growing on these trees. These apples are not harvested with a machine. People pick the apples and put them into a *bucket*. Then they tip the bucket of apples into a big box.

These people are busy picking pineapples.
They cut the pineapples off the plants.
Then a machine takes them to the truck.

Rice grows on farms, too.
It needs lots of water to grow.
When the rice is ready to be harvested,
the farmer lets the ground dry out.
Then the rice can be harvested.
Rice can be harvested with a machine
or by hand.

9

A machine can harvest a crop of *wheat*, too. The wheat goes into the back of a truck. The truck takes the wheat away.

A machine is helping this farmer to pick corn.
If she didn't have the machine,
she would need lots of people to help her.

After crops have been harvested,
they can be put away until they are needed.
Crops like apples are put in a cool place.
This helps them to stay fresh.
Some crops like corn, rice and wheat
can be put into a big building called a silo.

silo

Farmers can sell their crops
to lots of places once they are harvested.
Some crops are sold in shops.

Some crops are made into other foods.
Wheat can be made into bread.
Then the bread goes to a shop to be sold.

These crops are now ready for you to buy
and eat at home.

15

Picture glossary

bread	dry	rice
bucket	machine	silo
corn	pineapples	wheat

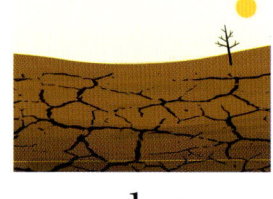